Also by Jerome Arthur

Antoine Farot and Swede
Down the Foggy Ruins of Time
Life Could be a Dream, Sweetheart
The Muttering Retreats
One and Two Halves
The Death of Soc Smith
The Finale of Seem
Oh, Hard Tuesday
Got no Secrets to Conceal

Brushes with Fame

A Memoir

Jerome Arthur

Brushes with Fame

Published by Jerome Arthur
P.O. Box 818
Santa Cruz, California 95061
831-425-8818
www.JeromeArthurNovelist.com
Jerome@JeromeArthurNovelist.com

Copyright © 2016 Jerome Arthur
ISBN: 978-1539430421

Acknowledgments

Thanks to Austin Comstock for editorial assistance. Also, thanks to Sherri and Steve Goodman for the cover art.

Dedicated to the Memory of Hats

Table of Contents

    Introduction…8
1. Bob Hatfield—Summer, 1959…11
2. Steven Spielberg—Spring, 1967…36
3. Michael Parks—Fall, 1977…47
4. Neil Young—Spring, 1983…62
5. Tom Lehrer—Winter, 1995…90
6. Nina Hartley—Spring, 2015…101
    Epilogue…112

Introduction

When I got the idea for this book, I only had four profiles in mind, the first four listed in the table of contents on the previous page. Then I started talking to some of my clients in the barber shop, and they convinced me that I should include the fifth and sixth names on the list. I listen to my clients. It's where I get my news. I have a lot in common with most of them. I'd say that probably ninety percent of my clientele is on my side (the left) of the political spectrum, some more liberal than others. So, when they tell me I should do something, I listen to them.

I've been telling some of these stories in the shop for years, so I decided, what the hell, why not write 'em down? I've got some disclaimers. The first is: when I quote any of the subjects of this book, those quotes may not be verbatim, but they will accurately convey the substance of the conversation. I have a good memory, but not that good.

These are not the kinds of profiles that one would find in magazines like *People* or *Us*. They are not meant to be "celebrity" profiles. They are simple vignettes that show where my path crossed the person's in the profile, and how my life was affected by the encounter. If these stories are about anybody, they are about me. And here's another disclaimer: I wouldn't, by any stretch of the imagination, claim to *know* any of my subjects. This is simply a tale of "six degrees of separation."

I'm not likely to attain even a scintilla of the fame in my lifetime that the subjects of my profiles have achieved; therefore, I'm writing about them and how my association, however small, with them has had an effect on my life. I think I learned something from all of them. Maybe I didn't learn how to be famous like they are, but that's all right, because I'm not really looking for fame. I'd rather have the fortune.

Bob Hatfield—Summer, 1959

I first met Bob Hatfield in June 1959. We were in Navy boot camp together, both of us in Company A for the first week. We stood next to each other when we fell into ranks. When I was doing weekend warrior duty over the previous nine months in my senior year at Cathedral High School, I learned that when you fall in for muster, tall guys line up on the right, and the rank tapers down on the left to the littlest guy. When you start marching, the big guys are out front. I didn't know it then, but I've since figured out that that's a military tactic. You want to show the enemy your biggest and (not always) meanest guys up front.
     So, what's all this got to do with me and Bob Hatfield in boot

camp? Well, for one thing at age eighteen, we were both exactly five feet nine inches tall, and when you're an eighteen-year-old kid just one weekend out of high school, you think you're bigger than you actually are, or at least you wish you were. For our age Bob and I were about average height. Both of us tried to line up with the taller guys. That's testosterone for you. We both knew that we were *about* the same height; we just didn't know the exact measurement. So, every time he and I would fall in, we'd try to get the spot on the right. We tried to beat each other by getting to muster early, and if we both got there at the same time we'd both protest,

"I'm taller'n you."

"No way, dude, I'm taller."

And on and on…till about the next day. We mustered and marched everywhere: first thing in the morning from the barracks to the mess hall, after chow back to the barracks, from the barracks to class, from class back to the mess hall, after chow to the grinder, after marching on the grinder back to the mess hall, after chow to study hall till 10 p.m., back to the barracks for taps. So, by the end of the first day of Bob and I fighting over who got to stand with the tall guys, the other boots right around us finally jumped in.

"Okay, you two guys get back-to-back here. We're go'n'a find out who's the tallest."

Well, nobody was the tallest. We were both exactly the same height. We flipped a coin and I won the toss. And so, we became friends.

I saw quite a bit of him throughout the rest of 85 Day School at Los Alamitos Naval Air Station even though I was taken out of Com-

Jerome Arthur

pany A after the first week and quartered to Company D. No matter. We were all in the same barracks, so I saw him and hung out with him a lot.

Once when I was shaving at a wash basin in the head, I heard someone singing in the shower around the corner.

"Para bailar la bamba! Para bailar la Bamba, se nesecita una poca de gracia…."

To my untrained ear, it sounded pretty damned good! It sounded as good as, if not better than, Ritchie himself. Then the guys started straggling out of the shower, and one of them was Bob.

"Hey, Hats. Who was singing in there?" I asked.

Bob had a tattoo on his forearm of a top hat and cane with the word "HATS" in fancy lettering arched over the top. That was the only nickname we ever knew him by. I recently looked at his Wikipedia entry and discovered that he was referred to throughout as Bobby, except where they gave his full name and where he was born. His son was even listed as Bobby junior. We never knew him by that nickname.

"I'll cop to it," he replied.

"Wow that sounded great! Good as Ritchie!"

"Yeah. Just watch me," he said with absolute confidence.

Besides doing weekend warrior stuff in my senior year, my other extra curricular activities included a couple of singing gigs. I laugh at the idea now. To my great disappointment, I never was much of a singer, even when I was a little kid. I was no candidate for the church choir.

In fall semester when I was working at Clifton's cafeteria, one of the other busboys, an older guy named Dick, wanted to start a trio. I thought my talents lay elsewhere, but Dick must have thought I had some potential as a singer because he wanted to start this trio, and he wanted me in it. He and I were the singers, and another kid named Sonny played the guitar. Dick was good, and he even taught me some things that made me a better singer.

We rehearsed "Autumn Leaves" for a month before Halloween, and then we performed it at the dance they had at the Olive Street Clifton's every year on Halloween. We also sang a rocker entitled "Don't Be Angry," a popular R&B tune four years earlier in 1954. It was a lot of fun, but in the end it wasn't very good. The bottom line was I couldn't carry a tune in a red Radio Flyer wagon. Still can't.

Brushes with Fame

Every year my high school, Cathedral High, an inner-city Catholic school two blocks north of Chinatown, put on a Spring Concert. The glee club, the band, and some individuals and small groups would perform. The Christian Brothers always encouraged the seniors to join the senior chorus and so I did. I only remember one song that we sang along with the glee club, "Wonderful! Wonderful!" I think it was only because there were so many other voices around me that you couldn't tell how bad I sounded. Well, so much for my "singing gigs."

So, it was with this background that I started talking with Hats and another one of the guys, a dude named Roger Uehara, about the possibility of putting together a trio. We didn't talk about it for long, and no trio was ever formed.

Jerome Arthur

In September we all went back to our reserve squadrons, and I went to barber college. I didn't see Hats again until spring of the following year. I was striking for the rate of Personnel Man, so I worked in the personnel office in my squadron. Being in that position afforded me many opportunities other weekend warriors didn't have, like getting advance notice on different things. One of those notices came from the Bureau of Personnel in Washington D.C. It said that weekend warriors could serve their active duty on the base where they were serving their reserve duty.

During 85 Day School, we took a two week cruise on board the aircraft carrier U.S.S. Kearsarge. When I stepped off that ship, I vowed to do anything to get out of going to sea when I went on active duty.

Brushes with Fame

The notice I got that day was my salvation from, and ticket out of, sea duty. I went ahead and signed up for the T.A.R. program (training and administration of reserves). The only difference between this and what I'd originally signed up for was that I had to do three years active duty instead of two. I figured that since Los Alamitos was only thirty-five miles from home, I could do the extra year standing on my head, so I signed up. I could also complete my course of study in barber school part-time, which I did.

The snack room in the building where my office was located was right in the center of the building. It separated my office from the personnel office. One Saturday when the weekend warriors were on the base, I went into the snack room to get a Snickers bar out of one of the candy machines. As I was putting my fifteen cents in the machine, Hats came through the room on his way to the base personnel office.

"Hey, Jerry," he said, when he saw me. "What's goin' on?"

"Hats! I ain't seen you since 85 Day School. What's up?"

"It's my weekend. Got'a go to the personnel office. What's up with you?"

"I'm on active duty. Workin' in the Nav.Cad./A.O.C. recruiting office right through that door," I said pointing at the door on the right.

"Oh, cool. I may be gettin' a record released, and I wan'a get yuh a copy."

"No kiddin'!"

"Yeah. Supposed to come out in Arizona."

"That is so cool! Hey, my office is right through that door. I'm here every day Tuesday through Saturday, eight to four-thirty."

"Okay. You'll hear from me," he said and went into the personnel office.

I went back to my office and didn't hear anything from him until a year later, and then it wasn't when he came to my office to give me a copy of a record he'd cut. It was at the Sigma Alpha Epsilon fraternity house just off Ocean Boulevard on one of the Places, 14th or something, in Long Beach.

In March I moved into an apartment in Long Beach with one of my Navy buddies, Chris Rope, who ac-tually was born and raised in Long Beach and was a Long Beach State dropout. He came to me in May and told me about a party scene at the Long Beach State frat. houses at the end of the school year.

Jerome Arthur

"Called T.G.I.O.," he said. "Wan'a go?"

"Absolutely! I don't know anybody in this town. Be a chance to meet some people."

And so, when the big night came, we went off to do some serious partying. The first frat. we went to was the Tau Kappa Epsilon house. I only bring this up because of its comic value to the story.

Chris and I and some of his friends were standing in a room next to a wall that had empty beer cans stacked from floor to ceiling. As we stood there drinking our beers, I noticed two guys wrestling in the hall and moving toward us. One was a middle age guy, probably forty or so, and the other was in his twenties. They were just horsing around, not really fighting. When they got into the room where we were, they ran smack into

Brushes with Fame

the wall lined with empties, and the cans all came tumbling down on them. We had to move out of the way so we wouldn't get rained on.

"Dr. Hardy," Chris said, pointing at the older guy. "Teaches poli. sci. at State. Young guy's one a' his grad. students."

Two years later I would see Dr. Hardy when I was working in Ernie Hanke's barber shop in Belmont Shore. He was one of Ernie's regular clients.

We finished our beers and moved on to the S.A.E. house. There was a band set up, but it was between sets, so the stage was vacant except for a microphone, a couple guitars, a tenor sax and a drum set. The band members were on a break. Chris introduced me to a whole new group of his friends. So, as we drank our beers, someone shouted from behind me,

Jerome Arthur

"Is that Jerry Fardette?"

Jerry was the nickname I went by until I was almost sixty years old. When I started using Jerome, I dropped the surname in favor of my middle name. And that's how I arrived at my pen name. I figure I'm in good company: Ray Charles, Billy Joel, Bonnie Bedilia, Dennis Franz, and best of all, Jon Stewart.

I turned around to see who it was, and to my surprise it was Bob Hatfield!

"Hats! What's happening? You in this fraternity?"

"Yeah! But I'm with the band, too. Doin' the vocals."

"Oh, that's cool! Still singin', huh?"

"Oh, yeah. Doin' a few gigs here and there."

Brushes with Fame

"What happened to the record deal in Arizona you told me about last year?"

"Never happened, but I'm still pluggin' away. Yuh oughta' come out and see my show in Santa Ana. I got a gig at The Black Derby. Group's called the Variations. We're good."

There it was again, Bob's certainty that he was going to make it in the music business. He had the same confidence he'd had two years ago when he came out of the shower and said,

"Watch me."

"Aw, too bad about the record deal not happenin'. But it's cool that you got a steady gig. Hey, I'm comin' out to see your show sometime."

"You still on active duty?"

"Got two more years to go. That day I saw you last year?"

"Yeah?"

Jerome Arthur

"I was just one month into my hitch then. Got two to go now."

Just about then, the members of the band started to take the stage, so we said our goodbyes and he joined them. Chris and I stuck around for one song, and I was once again really impressed. He was good, no question about it.

I never did make it out to The Black Derby, and I never actually talked to him or saw him in person and up close again. I've always wondered what he did to get out of doing his active duty in the Navy. The Wikipedia entry on him made no mention of any military service.

The next time I heard anything about Hats was when I was in my first full-time semester at Long Beach City College in the spring of 1963. And then I didn't know it was his voice I was listening to. I was in an English

Brushes with Fame

11A class. That was a five-unit class that included English 1A plus speech. I also had a California geography class and when the teacher started talking about John Steinbeck, the Salinas Valley and Monterey, I began reading his stuff, starting with *East of Eden,* followed by *Tortilla Flat* and *Cannery Row.*

I got really friendly with a woman in the English class, Sherry Matson. I wouldn't go so far as to say we were dating, but we did go out a few times. She was also reading some Steinbeck and that was how we connected. We both liked him, and we'd have extended discussions about his writing.

When Memorial Day rolled around, I suggested to her that we take a ride up to Monterey, check out the town, especially Cannery Row. She thought that was a great idea, so early

Jerome Arthur

Monday morning we took off from her parents' house and headed north on 101. I was driving a yellow 1962 Austin Healey Sprite. The top was down; the dashboard radio was blasting. Around Ventura, she suddenly turned the volume up on the radio and said,

"Here, listen to this. This is a couple fraternity brothers from Long Beach State. They sound like a black rhythm and blues band. The Righteous Brothers."

She quit talking and we listened to "Little Latin Lupe Lu." I had no idea that the tenor voice I was listening to was Hats.

In 1964 I was hanging with my big brother Jim at our parents' house watching T.V. I don't know where our parents were; they weren't there.

Unlike me, Jim could sing. He had a beautiful tenor voice. He was always more musical than I was. We

Brushes with Fame

both took piano lessons when we were little kids. I even took a little violin. But I just wasn't musical and he was. He didn't need the lessons. He learned to play guitar and piano by ear. I had a tin ear.

When he went to Glendale College he joined a fraternity and met a couple guys and the three of them formed a trio. They did Kingston Trio covers in a few spots around Glendale and Silver Lake. I remember going to see them at a place called the Red Lion over near Silver Lake. One of the guys in the trio, Emilio Delgado, moved to New York and ultimately got a permanent gig on *Sesame Street*. I just read a story in the paper that he lost his job playing the role of Luís. He started playing that role in 1971. I've seen him at least once on a *Law & Order* episode.

Jerome Arthur

But, getting back to my big brother Jim and his music. He was a big fan of Hoyt Axton, and I remember him liking a lot of the rhythm and blues that I liked when we were in high school.

So, this one night in 1964 we were watching The Andy Williams Show on the boob tube. He went down the list of different people who were his guests that night, and one of those acts was the Righteous Brothers. I remembered the name from the year before when I was with Sherry, but only vaguely. I still didn't know who they were, so when Hats and his partner, Bill Medley, took the stage, my jaw dropped. They sang, "You've Lost That Lovin' Feelin'."

Jim had gone to 85 Day School in 1958 so he was familiar with that program.

Brushes with Fame

"Wow, Jim! I was in 85 Day School with that guy!" I said, pointing at the T.V. screen.

"No kiddin'," he said. He was really excited and impressed. "That's great, man!"

This was a really cool bonding moment for my brother and me. We were never good buddies, especially when we were school age. In fact, from as far back as I can remember until we were stationed together at Los Alamitos, we had a bad case of sibling rivalry. I was glad that by the time we saw Hats on television we were able to hang out and have brotherly time together. We got plenty of time like that, but not enough. Jim died the same year as Hats. He was a year older.

In 1967, I ran into a mutual friend from 85 Day School named Jim Hildebrand at a bar I hung out at in Belmont Shore.

Jerome Arthur

"How about Hats?" he said as we sipped our beers.

"I was blown away a couple years ago when I saw him on Andy Williams. That was the first time I found out how big he was."

"I think I saw that same show 'cause that's about the same time I found out."

"Hey, his take on 'Unchained Melody' has got'a be the definitive version of the song."

"I agree," he said.

We had a couple more beers and went our separate ways. Bob just kept getting more popular.

In October 1992 my wife Janet and I had friends who gave us tickets to see the Righteous Brothers at the Circle Star Theater in San Carlos. It was a great show. When Bill Medley introduced "Unchained Melody," he said something like,

Brushes with Fame

"This next song is my little brother Bobby's song. Nobody does it better. 'Unchained Melody.'"

So, I guess Bobby it is, and I guess I should have referred to him that way, but I just never knew him by that name.

When the show was over, I tried to figure out how to get backstage to see if I could talk to Hats, but I never was any good at figuring stuff like that out, so we just drove back home to Santa Cruz that night. And that was the last time I ever saw Bobby Hatfield in the flesh.

My hometown of Santa Cruz used to have a classic car show called the Beach Street Revival that ran from the late seventies through the eighties and into the nineties. They always had an oldies band that played at the Cocoanut Grove on Saturday night of the event. In 1993 the Righteous Brothers was that band. Apparently they were the judges for a bikini contest that was held on the river bench lands in San Lorenzo Park where the cars were all on display. A friend of mine was there, and he later told me that he talked to both Bobby and Bill. He was that close. I had no idea they were in town, so I didn't make it to the event. That was really my last brush with Bob Hatfield and his fame.

In November 2003, I was saddened to read Bob's obituary in the newspaper. He was just sixty-three years old. He is the only one of my six profiles who is no longer with us, and I have dedicated this book to his memory.

Steven Spielberg—Spring, 1967

I never actually met Mr. Spielberg in the Creative Writing/Short Story class I took in my first semester of graduate school at Long Beach State College. He was one of fifteen students in the class. I did have some inter-action with him as I did with the other students when we read the short stories we wrote to the class. He wrote a story entitled "THE WORLD ISN'T READY FOR THEATRICAL DECLINE," and I still have a copy of it.

I was a twenty-six-year-old Navy veteran; he was a nineteen-year-old U.S.C. film school reject (their loss), but we in the class didn't know that at the time. However, I do believe that most of us could sense that we were in the presence a hall-of-famer in his rookie season. I think he might have been an English major even though we had a first-rate film school at Long Beach. I was an English major and aspiring novelist, and I took the class because I was ready to write some fiction after four years of essays and research papers on other writers, most notably, William Faulkner and Arthur Miller.

We were responsible for writing three short stories for the semester. When we finished writing a story, we went to the teacher, Dr. Foote, and told him how many pages it was. He gave us ditto masters matching the page count, and we would go home and type the story on the ditto masters. When we brought the story back to the teacher, he'd run off fifteen copies, bring them to class, and hand them out. We would then read the story to the class, and everybody would discuss it.

Jerome Arthur

By the end of the first month of class, I had written two stories, "Brain Tumor" and "Nickel Street" which I eventually published in a book I wrote called *Barber Shop Quartet.* Spielberg was in the class the day I read "Brain Tumor," and I remember his comment when I finished reading it. It was only one word, "Wow!" I took that to mean that he liked the story. I was so young and dumb, and I really didn't appreciate the comment as much as I should have, but now fifty years later, after seeing all of his many achievements worldwide, I am really grateful for the comment, and I have a great deal of respect for him.

The only time my name was ever mentioned in the same breath as Mr. Spielberg's was when I handed in my second story, "Nickel Street." When Dr. Foote brought the mimeographed copies to the class, he said,

Brushes with Fame

"This is really a good class. I've got Mr. Fardette's second story here, and I just now spoke long distance from Sausalito to Mr. Spielberg. He says he wants to write a story about the hippies on the houseboats there."

That was my second brush with fame. I'm sure he finished the class because I did see him on the day that I was in a student production in my Modern Drama class. I got involved in it because the teacher let us do that in lieu of taking the final. I remember going into the short story class pumped up from just coming offstage after participating in my first theatrical production. I look at it now and see how ridiculous I must have looked to the other students in the class, especially Steven Spielberg, who, I could see, was on a different level than the rest of us. I went into the class reciting lines from "A Spurt of Blood" a little three-

Jerome Arthur

minute play written by Antonin Artaud. What can I say? The production was a success and I ended up getting an A in the class. I only got a B in the short story class.

I had saved all the stories from the class in a manila folder that was about six inches thick with short stories. Some of the students had written two or three; I wrote the two I talked about here; I found only one written by Steven A. Spielberg. I'd actually saved all my lecture notes from freshman year through grad. school.

The next time I saw Mr. Spielberg's name was in the fall of 1970 when I was teaching Remedial English at Skyline College in San Bruno. I was working in a barber shop in Linda Mar Shopping Center in Pacifica Tuesday through Friday from three to six in the afternoon and all day Saturday. The teaching job was an evening school

Brushes with Fame

gig Monday through Thursday. My Remedial English class met Tuesday and Thursday from seven to nine-thirty.

When I got home at around ten o'clock one Thursday night (my wife, my infant daughter and I were living in El Granada on the San Mateo Coastside at the time), I was so beat that all I could do was sit down in my easy chair, fire up a doobie and watch the ten o'clock movie on channel 2.

So that's what I did on that Thursday night in the fall of 1970. The movie that was playing was *Duel* starring Dennis Weaver. As I watched the credits roll, I was astonished when I saw the director's name at the end of the credits: Steven Spielberg. I thought it was really a good movie, and I still think it's one of his best.

After that, I was so busy trying to make a living and raising a family.

Jerome Arthur
Those were the toddler years for our daughter, Kimberley. We didn't have time to go to movies, especially from 1970 until early 1973. In 1972 I opened my first barber shop in El Granada and I was starting to make some economic headway, but there were no movie theaters on the San Mateo Coastside, so we still weren't going to movies. That wouldn't happen until 1976 after we'd been back in Santa Cruz for a year. We were so busy moving and getting settled in 1975 that we missed *Jaws* when it came out. I wasn't really aware that it was his movie. Kimberley was only five and I was still busting my hump trying to make a living.

It wasn't until 1978 when Janet went back to work and Kimberley was eight years old that we started going to movies again. We saw *Raiders of the Lost Ark* and *E.T.* when they came out, and that's when I knew that I'd been in college, indeed been in the same class, with a bona fide superstar.

In 1985 I lost my lease on my barber shop and had to move into smaller quarters. In short, I had to downsize. It was then that I discovered that I still had the short story, "THE WORLD ISN'T READY FOR <u>THEATRICAL DECLINE</u>" as I was going through some old lecture notes from classes I'd taken at Long Beach State. That's when I discovered the manila folder full of stories from that Creative Writing class, and Spielberg's story was in among them.

When I'd tell people the story of how I was in the same classroom with Mr. Spielberg and show them the short story, they'd invariably tell me that I should try to get him to sign it. Readers will remember from my introduction that it was my clients who urged

Jerome Arthur

me to add the last two names to this memoir. I never was really keen on the idea of getting Mr. Spielberg's autograph, but after some months of my clients telling me to do it, I finally did. I wrote what I thought was a friendly letter and sent it with first class postage. A week later the letter was returned to me unopened in a larger envelope. The accompanying letter said, "This office does not accept unsolicited manuscripts."

I understand fully what the thinking behind that was, and I really didn't expect to be successful with my request, but the real insult came one week later when I received a five by eight manila envelope stuffed with E.T. Fan Club literature. The cover letter said, "Be the first in your neighborhood to join the E.T. Fan Club." The other literature in the packet consisted of glossy brochures offering Tshirts, coffee mugs and other paraphernalia. I packed everything back into the envelope it came in and re-sealed it with scotch tape. Then I put the whole packet in a larger manila envelope and sent a cover letter that said, "This office does not accept unsolicited manuscripts."

In my introduction I say that I've told some of these stories many times in my barber shop. This is one of them. And none of this is to say that I'm not a fan of much of Steven Spielberg's work. I think *Schindler's List* and *Munich* are two really excellent movies.

It is also my plan to send this book to all of the people profiled here (I'll send Bob's copy to Bill Medley), and I'm hoping I can get Mr. Spielberg's copy to him without it being returned to me unopened.

Michael Parks—Fall, 1977

This is the first profile of someone who was already famous when I met him, and he's the first one of the six to sit in my barber chair and get a haircut.

   I met Michael Parks when I was cutting hair at the Oak Chair Barber Shop in Santa Cruz, California. He was a walk-in and since I didn't have any appointments scheduled right then, I told him to sit down and I'd cut his hair. As soon as I wrote his name in my appointment book, I knew who he was. I remembered him from a T.V. show that he was the lead actor in eight years earlier, *Then Came Bronson.*

   I was wrapping things up at the Oak Chair, getting ready to move into the little haircutting studio I'd built into my one-car garage at home. I'd be moving to the Hair Hideaway on the Westside in just two weeks.

When I cut Michael's hair that first day I told him about my coming move. I already had cards printed with my new address. My phone number was the same. He said he'd call me when he was ready for another cut.

It took another two and a half months for him to get back to me, and then he was on a two-month schedule for the next year and a half. I cut his hair six times.

One of those times he brought in with him his son James and Jim's cousin Eric Entinman, and I cut their hair, too. All the time I was cutting Michael's hair, I thought he had a sister living in Ben Lomond, a small town on Highway 9 six miles up the mountain from Santa Cruz. I was thinking that would be Eric's mother, since he was introduced to me as Jim's cousin. When I checked Michael's IMDb biography, I discovered that he only had one sibling, a brother named Jimmy, and he died in 1968. So, I'm not sure now exactly what Eric's relationship to Michael and Jim was.

That day, I cut Michael's hair first and then James got in the chair. Eric was next after him. Michael said he had an errand to run and he'd be back before I finished the two haircuts. What I remember about that day was what Jim said to me.

"Yuh know, my dad says he really likes how you cut his hair. Says you're a real good barber."

"No, kiddin'. He really say that?"

"Yeah."

Jerome Arthur

That got me all pumped up for the day, and that was great. I always like to hear compliments like that.

Another time Michael told me he had done some work with Burt Reynolds at his dinner theater in Jupiter, Florida. And of course, every time he told me something like that, I'd repeat it to Janet at the dinner table, and she'd be thoroughly impressed.

I remember one time he told me one of his favorite actors to work with was John Carradine. He even did a fairly good impression of him. I liked his take on Carradine's acting style. I was impressed with his range as demonstrated in such mainstream Hollywood feature films as *Stagecoach*, *The Grapes of Wrath* and *Myra Breckinridge*. Then he'd turn around and play roles in dozens, if not hundreds, of low budget horror films. The consummate professional actor.

Brushes with Fame

What I remember most about that year and a half of cutting his hair was Michael's last haircut with me. It was in the spring of 1979. In the fall of '78, Janet had gotten a half-time teaching job at Bonny Doon Elementary School in the Santa Cruz mountains. A couple years later it turned into a full-time tenure-track job, and she eventually retired from there after thirty years in the classroom.

This part-time gig was a special ed. job. She was a resource specialist, and because it was only part-time, she just went to the campus in the morning. She usually got home around noon.

Michael's appointment with me on that day was at 9:30 in the morning. I had another three cuts after him, and I finished up at about the time Janet got home from work. She pulled in the driveway as I was cleaning up my work station. She popped her head in the door.

"Wan'a go with me to the toy store in the Cooper House?"

The Cooper House was the old court house that had been converted into a restaurant (the Wild Thyme) and bar (the Oak Room) with live music weekends on the front patio, and boutique shops (leather, jewelry, women's apparel) on the upper two floors. Behind the restaurant, also on the ground floor by the side entrance, was a flower shop and a toy store.

That building was the center of town in the seventies and eighties, and then in 1989 we had the Loma Prieta earthquake. For reasons I have yet to figure out, the owner of the property got a demolition permit, and he took the wrecking ball to the building one week after the quake. I was there the first day of the demolition, and the

Brushes with Fame

other hundred or so people and I who were there, cheered when the wrecking ball bounced off the upper stories three times before it did any damage on the fourth try. Ten days after the demolition, there was still a pile of rubble fifteen feet high. That was one building that could have been and should have been saved.

"Sure," I said to Janet. "I'll go have a beer in the Oak Room while you're in the toy store."

She went into the house, and I finished cleaning up the shop. As I was locking up, she came back out, and we got in the car and headed down to the Cooper House. Since it was Tuesday, there wasn't much happening. There was no music on the patio and the restaurant and bar were pretty quiet.

Janet went back to the toy store, and I went into the Oak Room. There were only four other people in the room and three of them were sitting on barstools along the long side of the L toward the back. Michael Parks was standing on the short side of the L, and he was mostly entertaining the three people sitting in a line. They were a young man and two young women. I sat down next to the second woman. I found out later that the man and the first woman were a couple, and they were all three together.

Michael was carrying on, and he didn't even notice that I'd sat down at the bar. After the bartender took my beer order, the woman I was sitting next to said to me,

"Know who that is?"

She was wide-eyed.

"In fact, I do," I said. "Watch this." Then to Michael, "Nice haircut yuh got there."

Brushes with Fame

"Hey, Jerry. You bet. I got a good barber."

And then he went back to entertaining the couple, and I started talking to the woman next to me. She was really quite beautiful. It was just about then that Janet came into the bar. She walked right up to me and gently back-handed me on the upper arm.

"So, what cha doing here?" she said, kiddingly, showing what I thought was exaggerated jealousy, but she told me later that she wasn't exaggerating one iota.

At that the other woman said to the woman I was talking to in a semi-whisper, "That's his wife."

Michael picked up on that right away and said to me,

"Is she your wife?"

"Yeah," I said.

He came over, and I introduced him to Janet. We chit chatted some. I

Jerome Arthur

think he told her something about what a good barber I was, and then he said something that I always considered to be the kiss of death.

"Hey, why don't you guys come down to my condo in Pájaro Dunes. We can soak in the hot tub, put some steaks on the barbecue. Wha' da yuh say?"

Janet said without hesitation, "Sure, when do you want us to come down?"

"How 'bout tomorrow night."

"'Sounds great! How do we get there?"

"I'll call Jerry in the morning and give him directions. How's eight o'clock sound?"

"Great! We'll be there."

I was starting to feel like the odd man out of that conversation. Those two had set it all up on their own.

Brushes with Fame

We left the bar and went home so we'd be there when our eight-year-old daughter got home from school. As soon as she did get home, Janet took her to Leask's, our local department store on the Pacific Garden Mall. She bought a new bathing suit for the big night. When she got home and modeled it for me, she said,

"The question is, can a thirty-five-year-old woman lose twenty pounds in twenty-four hours."

She was really excited, so excited, in fact, that the next day she told her fellow teachers and the school secretary, who was a big Michael Parks fan, about the big night.

"Maybe Burt and Sally will be there," she told me she told her co-workers.

Of course, she was only kidding, but that's Janet. She gets really exited when it comes to holiday celebrations or meeting famous people and having the opportunity to socialize with them. That's why I love her so much.

The next morning, I went out to the shop and found a message on my answering device from Michael Parks. The message was an apology for not being able to keep the date. He said he had to go down south and that he'd be gone for a while, but that Janet and I definitely had a rain check when he got back.

That was the last time I heard his voice until I saw him in a movie called *Escape from Bogen County* opposite Jaclyn Smith. I didn't see it until mid 1979, but its original theatrical release was October 1977, one month after I started cutting his hair.

One time a couple/three years ago, I was flipping through the channels on the television, and suddenly

Brushes with Fame

there he was on the screen acting a scene in a movie. I clicked on the guide and saw that I was watching *Kill Bill Vol. 1*. The last time I saw him on the big screen was when Janet and I went to a Sunday matinee and saw *Django Unchained*. I recently saw him in *The Assassination of Jesse James by the Coward Robert Ford*, which I rented from Netflix. He doesn't seem to have lost his touch. He's a really good actor.

    That day in the bar was the last time I saw Michael in person, but that's not where my story about him ended. Before we got out of the bar that day, I gave my card to the couple and the young woman I was talking to. She eventually came in a couple times for haircuts. The first time she told me she'd hung with Michael that whole day and had a great time. The second time I cut her hair, I asked her if she'd seen him since her last cut. She said no she hadn't, and that was the end of the story for me.

The most important thing to happen to me shortly after Michael quit coming to my shop was that I started working in earnest on the first book I published, *The Muttering Retreats*. I don't know what influence, if any, my encounter with him had on my writing, but it does seem coincidental that I was so inspired so soon after that episode.

Neil Young—Spring 1983

Where to begin a discussion about my time cutting Neil Young's hair. There was one false start in the process. He came to me through another one of my clients, David Cline. He was Neil's personal manager at the time. I had just moved my business into a little California bungalow in downtown Santa Cruz. One day I got a call from David, and he wanted to schedule an appointment for Neil, so I put him in my book for the next day. About an hour before the scheduled time, David called me to cancel the appointment. They were in Capitola, another Santa Cruz County beach town five miles down the coast. He said they couldn't make it because Neil was checking out some chrome for one of his classic cars, and they would be a while longer than they first thought.

I had been hearing about Neil for some time from David and other friends of mine who were fans, but up to that moment I didn't know a lot about him. I didn't have any of his records. I don't know why I was so remiss. I *was* a fan of Bob Dylan, Van Morrison, the Beatles, Leon Russell, and even Dire Straits, a fairly new band at that time. I had albums by every one of those artists and more. I should have already had at least some of Neil's records.

I was only in the bungalow for six months before the city made me move because the house was zoned residential, and they didn't want me running a business there. I went to work with my friend Jan Pendleton at Jan's Barber Shoppe in the Sash Mill,

Jerome Arthur

a shopping area just outside of downtown. I left her after six months to buy Frank Minuti's Palace Barber Shop on Cedar Street. I redecorated the place and made it into a two-station hair styling salon that I called Jerry the Barber & Co. It was in this shop that I cut Neil Young's hair for the next three years.

In the Spring of 1982, David called me and set up an appointment for Neil's son Ben to get a haircut. Pegi, Neil's wife and Ben's mom, brought him to the shop, and as I was cutting his hair, Pegi said,

"We've been wanting to come to you for a while. R.J.'s been telling us about you for a long time."

R.J. was Roger LeGrande, another one of my clients. He and Pegi were friends from high school.

So, I cut Ben's hair that day, and they went along their way. At that time my schedule ran from ten to noon and three to six in the afternoon weekdays, nine to noon on Saturday. I had a live answering service, and when I got back to the shop in the afternoon, I'd call them to see if anybody had called while I was out. Well, this one time several months after I'd cut Ben's hair, the operator at Quicksilver told me there was a call from Neil Young. I took the phone number down and called him. The voice at the other end of the line said,

"Hello."
"Hi, Neil?"
"Yeah?"

He dragged the word out ever so slightly, so that it really did sound like a question, but the unspoken question was, "Who the hell're you?" There wasn't much caller I.D. in those days, so it would've been a legitimate question. I have since changed the way I

Jerome Arthur

greet people when I'm calling them. I still address the person I'm calling first. My name comes next, as in, "Hi, Neil? This is Jerome at Surf City Barber Shop."

"This is Jerry the Barber. You called me earlier. I'm getting back to you."

"Oh, hey, hi, Jerry. Yuh got any openings for a haircut."

"For you? Or Ben?"

"It's for me this time."

"Okay, I could do it tomorrow at 3:30."

"That sounds good. I'll be there."

So, there it was. I was finally going to meet Neil Young. He showed up the next day with his good buddy, maybe his best friend, Jim Mazzio. I didn't meet Jim that first day. He just came in, sat down in a waiting chair and read a magazine while I worked on Neil's hair.

Someone always accompanied Neil when he came for haircuts. He never came in alone. Sometimes there would be as many as four guys. They never said anything; Neil never introduced them; they always sat in the waiting area of my shop and read magazines. It was a comfortable waiting area in a cozy shop with two barn wood styling booths in the big plate glass window in front. Between the booths and the back wall was a carpeted area where I had a cable reel and an old chest for tables, and four oak captains chairs.

I eventually did meet and talk to Maz because he was with Neil most often. In fact, I even cut his hair a couple times. The first time I asked him how he came to be friends with Neil Young.

Jerome Arthur

"I used to do light shows for Moby Grape, Buffalo Springfield and other groups. I worked with Buffalo Springfield a lot, and that's how I got to know Neil."

He had other stories to tell, but more of that later.

When Neil finally sat down in my chair, I asked him how he wanted his haircut.

"Gi'me a computer cut. I'm doin' an album about computers."

"What's a computer cut?"

"I don't know," he said jokingly. "Just give me a good haircut."

"I'll make yuh look like a real yuppie. How's 'zat sound?"

"Great! Do it!"

The album he was making was *Trans,* and the first haircut I gave him can be seen on the inner sleeve of the record. I don't mind saying it's a damn good haircut, one any eighties-yuppie would be proud of.

I didn't see him again for another five months, and when he came back the second time, he had another specific request.

"You do rockabilly?"

"You kiddin'? I learned how to cut hair doin' rockabilly. Sit down."

That haircut appears on the front cover of the *Everybody's Rockin'/Neil and the Shocking Pinks* album. Eat your hearts out, all you rockabillies from Carl Perkins to Brian Setser. I'm proud of some of the work I do in the barber shop. It's the one time that I feel like a sculptor, especially when I'm using shears (shears not clippers) over the comb on a medium/short men's haircut. It's also a lot of fun to section off women's hair that's shoulder-length or shorter and give the lady a fashionable hairstyle.

Jerome Arthur

But I digress once again. Back to how Neil's hair for the next couple years was my responsibility. Sometimes Neil would come in for just his cut, and other times he'd bring Ben with him and I'd do both of them.

The second time Maz sat in my chair, he told me Neil was an avid board sailor. Maz lived down by the yacht harbor, and he had a sailboat in a slip there.

"I'll take Neil and his board on my boat out in the bay. He throws his board in the water, catches the wind and sails around."

"You a board sailor, too?"

"No way."

"What're you doin' while Neil sails around?"

"I'm kicked back in the boat drinkin' an ice-cold beer. Put the sail down and drift around. Got power if I

Brushes with Fame

need it. I ain't gettin' in that cold water for anything. No way."

It was sometime around Neil's third visit that my sound system went on the fritz. To call it a "sound system" is an exaggeration. I am not an audiophile, and I have never been a great collector of records. Before compact discs came along, the only record collection I had was my Fats Domino forty-fives when I was fourteen years old. Oh, yeah, and when I was in my early thirties, I started collecting used albums that I bought at Logos, our local used book store. They also carry used records that they sell for a quarter apiece.

The sound system I refer to here is an old Packard Bell tube radio that my dad gave me when I graduated from high school. It was a shiny black plastic oblong cube with two knobs and a dial with a white plastic grill

Jerome Arthur

covering the speaker. Two years after I got it, I traded a cabinet maker a few haircuts and some cash for him to build me a maple cabinet. It served me well in all four of the barber shops I'd owned since 1972. It finally died in 1983, and I brought the turntable I had at home down to the shop and started playing the meager selection of albums I'd bought at Logos. The radio is presently on display in my barber shop. This all happened shortly after I started cutting Neil's hair.

"Hey, Neil," I said, a little embarrassed. "I'm starting to play albums in here, and yuh know, I don't have any of your records, and I'd like to get them to play in the shop. My radio finally gave up the ghost."

"You want my records? I can give yuh all of 'em."

Brushes with Fame

"No, no. I don't want yuh to give 'em to me. I wan'a trade yuh haircuts for 'em."

At that time record albums were going for about seven bucks. I was charging fourteen for haircuts, so I told him,

"Bring in two albums every time I cut your hair. Starting now. Don't give me any money today. Next time you come, bring four albums, two for this cut and two for your next cut. That sound cool?"

"That sounds very cool. You got it."

We made that deal on a Friday. On Tuesday I got a phone call from a woman who identified herself as Neil Young's administrative assistant.

"Could I get your mailing address. Neil has asked me to U.P.S. some albums down to you."

Jerome Arthur

"Yeah, sure," I said and gave her my address.

By the end of the week, U.P.S. delivered eleven albums to me, all autographed. There were nine single L.P.s, two double L.P. sets. *Trans* and *Everybody's Rockin'* were among them. I framed *Everybody's Rockin'* and *After the Gold Rush* and hung them on the wall in my barber shop. I point to the rockabilly album when I brag about my work. Neil signed the *...Gold Rush* album, "to Jerry," which I thought was pretty cool. Taped inside the clear plastic dust jacket of the album on top of the stack were two tickets to an upcoming show he was doing at the Catalyst, a small club in Santa Cruz that was a bowling alley in its original incarnation.

That was right when C.D. technology was taking off, and it wasn't long after that that I got a compact disc player and started my collection. Now, even in this time of streaming, Pandora, Spotify, and who knows what else, it's still how I listen to music.

So, about the show that I got tickets for, I invited another one of my clients, Jimmy Knier, a friend of David Cline, to come with me to the concert. The Catalyst isn't the snazziest place to see a concert, even though they attract top notch acts like Willie Nelson, Pearl Jam, even the Grateful Dead, and of course, Neil Young. But it's like I said before, it's a former bowling alley, and it's got the acoustics of a bowling alley, even though they installed baffles in the ceiling and around the stage.

Jim and I went to the concert, and it was good in spite of the acoustics. Nils Lofgren was playing lead guitar and he was good. He was quite amazing, playing guitar and doing gymnastics at the same time. The only other guy I saw do the same kind of workout at a rock 'n' roll concert was Mick Jagger in the movie, *Let's Spend the Night Together* in 1982.

I'm not crazy about going to a live concert. I have a hard time understanding the lyrics. It seems that the electric instruments drown out the words, and I think the words are the most important part of any composition, prose, poetry or song. I like studio albums better because you can understand the words. That night at the Catalyst, Neil put on a good show, but I found myself repeatedly asking Jim what song we were listening to.

Neil made an appointment in May 1985. When he showed up, he had four or five guys with him. I can't remember the exact number. The difference between this time and those other times when he had guys with him was that this time he introduced me to one of the group.

"Hey, Jerry! I want you to meet Rufus Thibodeaux!"

"Hello, Jerry," he said sticking out his hand and giving me a good firm handshake.

"Hey, Rufus. How's it goin', man?"

It was another beautiful Friday in Santa Cruz. The sun was shining; Warmth, our local jazz band led by Don McCaslin, was playing live at the Cooper House; you could hear the sax licks from the sidewalk in front of the shop; it couldn't have been nicer.

"This looks like a pleasant little town yuh got here," Rufus said. "I'd like to look around."

"Just go straight on this street right here," I said, pointing to Church Street. "One block to the Mall. Go left, go right, or just hang where yuh are.

Jerome Arthur

You'll dig it. I'll be finished with Neil in half an hour."

They all left, and I started working on Neil's hair.

"Rufus a musician?" I asked when I settled into doing the cut.

"Yeah. Fiddle player. Go'n'a play fiddle on my next album."

"Cool."

The guys came back when I was finished cutting Neil's hair and they all left.

The next time I saw Neil was a couple months later, only it wasn't live in the flesh. One Saturday in July, I got home from the shop at a little after twelve noon. As long as I've owned my own shop, I never have liked to work past noon on Saturday. I've said over the years that that's when my weekend starts. That Saturday when I walked in the back door, Janet was watching T.V. in the living room and she shouted out to me,

"Hey, Jer, you've got'a see this!"

I dropped my towels on top of the washing machine and went into the living room.

"It's something called Live Aid. It's concerts all over the world with all these different bands. They were at Wembley earlier; Philadelphia right now; they're go'n'a come out to the West Coast later and Japan after that. Looks like Phil Collins is go'n'a be at all of 'em. So far he's been at Wembley and here. This band that's playing right now is called Queen, and this lead singer is good."

"Wow! That sounds really cool! I'll be right back in. Le'me put my towels in the machine," I said and headed back to the service porch.

Jerome Arthur

Just as I finished getting the towels in the machine and got it going, Janet said,

"They just went to commercial, and they announced Neil Young up next."

"Be right there," I said and went into our room, unpacked my bag, and got into something comfortable.

By the time I got into the living room, Neil was already playing with his country band, The International Harvesters. Well into the song, Rufus stepped out front and did a fiddle solo.

"Hey, Babe, I just met that guy a couple months ago!" I said. "That's Rufus Thibodeaux!"

"You've got such a great job," Janet said. "You meet the most interesting people."

"I can't help it if I'm lucky," I quoted Dylan.

Brushes with Fame

"He's really a good violin player."

Neil's next haircut was in September. He pulled up in his '57 Cadillac, and when he got out of the car, he had the *Old Ways* album in his hand. That's the only album of his that I have that's not autographed. He just handed it to me, and I didn't think to ask him to sign it. That's also the album that Rufus plays on, along with a lot of other music superstars, including Waylon Jennings, Willie Nelson and Béla Fleck.

The front cover of *Rolling Stone* magazine, May 8, 1986 featured an interview with the Everly Brothers. I was always an Everly Brothers fan since my teen years, so I read the interview.

The interviewer asked them where they disappeared to after 1962, and one of them responded that he and

Jerome Arthur

his brother had gotten burned out from all the celebrity, and they decided to go down to New Orleans and dig into their musical roots. The other brother talked about going up into the bayou country and hooking up with Rufus Thibodeaux, and that's where they stayed for a while jamming with Rufus and some of his Cajun brothers. I just thought it was so cool that I got to meet a music legend.

Neil came into my shop one more time in summer of '86. I'd lost my lease on the barber shop at the beginning of the year, and not finding a new commercial spot downtown, I decided to go underground, and I moved back into my bungalow on Center Street. I kept the shutters closed, and my clients had to knock on my door before I'd let them in. That's where I was working the last time I saw Neil Young. I scheduled Ben for a haircut

Brushes with Fame

one beautiful Sunday morning in late June. It was the only cut I had scheduled that day.

I was standing out on my front porch waiting for them to arrive. Neil pulled up in the van they had customized for Ben's disability. A gray-haired guy with a beard was riding shotgun. As soon as the van came to a complete stop, he jumped out and came right up to me with his right hand extended.

"Hi, I'm Russ," he said.

"I'm Jerry. Nice to meet yuh, Russ."

"You got a john in there? Had too much coffee this mornin'."

"Yeah, it's right there," I said, pointing into my open front door.

As I got Ben set up for his haircut, Russ came out of the bathroom and into the room where I was working.

Jerome Arthur

"This looks like a pretty little town. I wan'a look around."

"Okay," I said. "Just go two doors up here to the parking lot. Then cut through the lot, and go one more block over to Pacific Avenue, the Mall. Take a left there and check it out."

"Is Russ a musician like Rufus?" I asked Neil after he was gone.

"No, Russ is actually a dancer and actor. He's been in about sixty Hollywood feature films."

"Really?"

"Really. You ever see *West Side Story*?"

"No! Don't tell me! That's Russ Tamblyn?"

"Yup, that's Russ Tamblyn."

"Wow! That is so cool! I was a big fan a' his when I was a teenager. You doin' somethin' musical with him?"

Brushes with Fame

"Yeah. I'm doing a video for M.T.V., and there's some dancing in it. I don't dance, so we're shooting me with my guitar from here up." He put his hands, palms up, down by his waste. "And then it's Russ from here down," still indicating his waist with his hands. "We're doin' it on the steps of the Bank of America building in San Francisco."

"Pretty cool," I said.

And then came the bad news.

"I'll drop off a copy next time I come down to hang out with Maz."

"Great! If I'm not here, just drop it in my mail slot."

But I knew instinctively that I'd probably never see that video, and in fact that was the last time I saw him. Shades of Michael Parks when he invited me and Janet to his place for steaks on the barbecue and soaking in the hot tub. That's always the way it is in the hair business. There are three things you never want to hear from a client. "You're always go'n'a be my haircutter." The second is, "Come on up to my place for dinner." And the third, "I've got this really cool thing and I want you to have a copy."

That's usually the end.

"Did you see the interview with the Everly Brothers in Rolling Stone last month?" I said, changing the subject.

"No, was it good?"

"Excellent. They talked about going up in the bayou country with Rufus Thibodeaux in the early sixties. It was so cool. 'Course I've always been an Everly Brothers fan."

"Yeah, they're good."

I finished cutting Ben's hair and Russ came back.

"What a nifty town you live in here!" he said.

Brushes with Fame

"We live in paradise. Yuh oughta' come back sometime. Get a haircut."

"That sounds great. I might do it," he said.

And that was the last time I ever saw him, Neil, Ben, Maz or anybody else I'd ever seen in my barber shop who ever came in with Neil Young. I actually did see Maz a couple times cruising up Pacific Avenue in his classic Chevy Sedan Delivery, but that was a long time ago.

What a great experience it was working with Neil and his son. I met interesting and talented people, and I got a cool collection of autographed L.P.s. And there's that intangible something that influences creativity. It was one year later, almost to the day, that I bought my first computer and really started writing in earnest. I had first drafts of two manuscripts that I'd written on the typewriter during the time I was cutting Michael Parks's hair. When I got the computer in 1986, I promptly wrote three more first drafts, and I transcribed the two typewritten ones into my hard drive. All of this before 1990. And it all started happening immediately following my dealings with Neil and the discovery of the Spielberg short story. I think those two events motivated me.

Tom Lehrer—Winter, 1995

"Sure, I got an open spot tomorrow afternoon at 3:30. What's your name? And give me your phone number, too."

"Tom Lehrer," he said and gave me a number.

This was my first exchange with Tom, and you can believe, my jaw fairly dropped when he said his name. I was a fan in the early sixties when he was at the height of his musical career. He's the only person I'm writing about here whom I was a fan of before I met him. Chris Rope, my first roommate and Navy buddy, the same guy I was with the last time I talked to Bob Hatfield, introduced me to Tom's music. He had a couple of his records, and when he played them for me I became a fan.

"This guy's a Harvard mathematician," Chris said after we listened to "Fight Fiercely, Harvard." "They say he's in trouble with his colleagues at the college. If it's true, it sounds like they don't have much of a sense of humor."

I was still on active duty with the Navy and hadn't been to college yet, so I really didn't have an opinion on the subject, but by the time I got to graduate school at Long Beach State, I could see how Tom Lehrer might be in trouble with other Harvard professors and administrators, especially administrators. It took three attempts for me to pass my comprehensives to get my M.A. degree in English, and it was all political as far as I could see. I had this feeling that it was beneath the dignity of those academics to consider having

Jerome Arthur

a lowly barber, a tradesman, join them in the ivory tower where they lived. You see, I had this crazy idea that I wanted to be a junior college English teacher.

Tom has this routine in his live shows where he tells the audience he doesn't "have to do this for a living. I could make $3,000 a year just teaching." And I can see where some college professors would be offended by such talk.

I wasn't absolutely sure it was the same guy who'd just made an appointment with me. In 1993 I finally got my barber shop set up in a permanent location. It's where I am today and where I'll probably end up dying. I tell my clients, "Yuh wan'a hope ye're not gettin' a haircut on the day I die, 'cause you'll have to give me mouth-to-mouth resuscitation so I can finish the cut." Another thing I like to

Brushes with Fame

tell them when they ask me who's going to cut their hair when I retire, "In order to retire, you have to have worked. What I do in the barber shop isn't work. I'm hangin' out with my best friends for forty-five minutes and when they leave, they gi'me money." And the best part of it is the talk, not the haircut. My hands are doing the cutting; my mind is elsewhere. The shop name was still Jerry the Barber, but by 1997 I changed that to Surf City Barber Shop, and I started calling myself Jerome, the name I was given at birth.

When Tom came in for his haircut the next day, the first thing I asked him when he sat down in the chair was,

"Are you the same Tom Lehrer who wrote "Poisoning Pigeons in the Park"?

Jerome Arthur

If I remember correctly, he held up his right index finger and replied,

"1959."

I was so delighted I had this guy in my chair that I was actually speechless. I don't think I said much more that day other than to ask him who recommended me to him, and to tell him what a great fan of his I was.

In 1972 he started teaching classes at U.C. Santa Cruz. He came here for the winter and spring quarters. He'd go back to Cambridge for summer and fall. One of his U.C.S.C. colleagues, Todd Newberry was the guy who sent him to me.

There really was no reason why I should be so star struck. After all, Tom Lehrer was the third famous person I'd had in my chair. I think it was because I was familiar with his work before I met him, and was already a fan, whereas I wasn't all that familiar

Brushes with Fame

with Michael's and Neil's work before I knew them.

Tom only got four haircuts from me over a six-month period, winter and spring quarters, 1995. I was a little more relaxed by the second appointment, comfortable enough to ask him questions.

"Back when you were making music, there was a rumor going around that you were not in good standing with your colleagues at Harvard because of how you used to poke fun at them and academia in general. Was that true?"

"Absolutely not true, but when we heard the rumor, we promoted it. I think it sold a lot of records."

"Who's the big name in political and social satire today, Mark Russell?"

"Oh, no. The one I think is the best is Randy Newman."

Jerome Arthur

"All right! He's one of my favorites. "Sail Away," "Political Science." He's got a lota' great songs."

One of the classes Tom taught at Santa Cruz was in the theater arts department. As I understood it, the class consisted of four days of rehearsals (Monday through Thursday), and then on Friday Tom and his class put on a live performance in the fireside lounge at Stevenson College. Tom chose lines from Broadway musicals, and he played the music on the piano while the students sang the lines and danced.

"Whatever happened to that class?" I asked him.

"Enrollments went down, and it went away."

He really impressed me the time he came in just as I was finishing up the cut before him. After that client paid me and left, I turned to Tom and said,

Brushes with Fame

"Dr. Lehrer. You're next."

"Ah, but I don't have a Ph.D. degree."

"I actually like that better," I said. "Have a seat."

Tom usually played it straight when he was in my shop. I'm sure he must have come up with some witty aphorisms, but I can't remember any of them. I'm that way with jokes, too. I just remember him coming in the shop, getting his hair cut and leaving. I was surprised one time when he gave me a C.D., *Songs and More Songs by Tom Lehrer*. The liner notes were written by Dr. Demento, and, I believe, were nominated for a Grammy award.

Summer came and Tom went back to Cambridge, and when he came back to Santa Cruz, which I know he did, he went somewhere else for his haircuts. A couple years ago, I saw him walking past my front window.

Jerome Arthur

Otherwise, I haven't seen him since then. Todd Newberry is still a regular customer in my shop. I see him every three weeks, and like all my other clients, he is booked with me through the end of the year.

"Have you seen Tom Lehrer lately," I asked Todd recently.

"Yes," he said. "There have been quite a few retirements recently. That's where I usually see him, and he's just as witty as ever."

In each of these profiles I've tried to show how being acquainted with these people has somehow enriched my life. With Tom Lehrer it's hard to pinpoint what single thing about knowing him might have made my life richer. It's really everything that came before I met him that's made the impact. I think with him, it's more of a cumulative thing—fifty-five years of listening to and being entertained by his music and his monologues between the songs.

Nina Hartley—Spring, 2015

This portrait has the lightest brush stroke of any that I've tried to paint here with my words. I haven't yet made Nina Hartley's acquaintance in person. Because of logistics, we haven't been able to meet, but I did have a featherlike brush with her fame, and here's the story.

She'd come into my consciousness through her cousin, Max Copperman. I'd been cutting his hair for twenty-five years when he came in one Saturday morning and asked me,

"You know who Nina Hartley is?"

The name sounded familiar, but I wasn't sure where I'd heard it.

"'Sounds very familiar. How would I know her?"

Jerome Arthur

"She's an adult film star."

"Okay. Yeah. It's coming to me now."

"She's played in one Hollywood feature film, *Boogie Nights*."

As soon as he said that, I knew exactly who she was. Janet and I are avid movie goers and that's one we saw at one of our Sunday matinees. We both like Mark Wahlberg, and we were also Burt Reynolds fans when he was hanging with Sally Fields. It was mostly because of her that we liked him. But I digress. I'll go see Julianne Moore in any movie she's in. *Fargo* is my second favorite movie of all time, right behind *Casablanca*, so William H. Macy is another favorite for Janet and me.

"Of course! That's where I recognized the name! I saw that movie twice, once in the theater, and I rented it from Netflix for a second look. So, what about her?"

"She was at my house last night."

"Oh, really? What's up with that?"

"She's my cousin. She's written a book, and she was at a book signing at Camouflage, and I drove her there."

Camouflage is a store on Pacific Avenue. They sell clothing in the front of the store, mostly sexy under garments for women. In the back it's all pornography: sex toys, movies, and books like *Nina Hartley's Guide to Total Sex*. And so, she was there selling and signing her book.

"Wow! That's pretty cool! What kind of a crowd did she draw? Who was there?"

"It was a full house. I only saw about three guys in the audience. They were mostly young women. There didn't seem to be many who looked like they were over thirty. One of the young women asked Mitzi to sign her breast, and she did."

Max referred to her by the nickname he'd known her by since they were kids, Mitzi.

"What does her family think about what she does?"

I wasn't getting it right then. I hadn't seen a whole lot of porn in my life, but what I did see I liked. I'd seen some eight-millimeter stuff when I was in the Navy and when I was working in Sam Tellez's Manor Barber Shop in Pacifica. Sam used to have a good supply of illegal fireworks around the Fourth of July, and a library of some fairly decent pornography year-round in his backroom. But that was all before 1972, which was the year that pornography became legal.

Brushes with Fame

Janet and I went with friends to see *Deep Throat* and *Behind the Green Door* a couple years after they came out, and *The Devil in Miss Jones* followed those two. A side note here: after I started talking to my other clients about Max and Nina, one of my client's, a guy named Bill Lipson, told me he lived in a bungalow court in Hollywood, and one of his neighbors was Georgina Spelvin, the title character in *The Devil in Miss Jones*. He told me he's still in touch with her and some of the other neighbors in the court.

That first time Max told me about Nina being his cousin, I was maybe halfway through writing my ninth novel, *Oh, Hard Tuesday*. This is a mystery about a missing coed whose aunt hires a private investigator to find her. When he finally does track her down, he learns that she is working with one of her college classmates as a prostitute.

I thought it would be a great idea to work Nina into my plot, so I started doing research on her, looking for an angle to tie her into the story somehow. I asked Max how she got into adult entertainment, and he told me she started out working as a dancer. The next step I took was to Google her name, and I learned from her Wikipedia page that she first got star-ted with the Mitchell brothers in San Francisco.

So, I went ahead and brought her into my story by having the missing coed tell the detective that her manager had made a demo video of her and her fellow prostitute performing on film. She tells the detective that they interviewed with the Mitchell brothers, and while they were there, they got to meet Nina Hartley.

Brushes with Fame

The time frame for the book was the two weeks on either side of the Loma Prieta earthquake. In my research I learned that Nina had started her career five years before that event. The coed tells the detective,

"She's a rising star in the adult film industry."

And so, I worked her into the story. When I had a first draft of the pages where her name appears, I printed them and brought them to the shop the next time I cut Max's hair.

"Here, check this out," I said, handing him the pages.

He read them and when he finished he said,

"Can I keep this?"

"Of course. That's why I gave 'em to yuh."

"I want her to see this. I think she'll like it."

Jerome Arthur

"That's why I gave 'em to yuh," I repeated with a little more emphasis.

When I finished the book and published it, I comped Max and Nina copies. The next time Max came in for his haircut, he handed me a manila envelope that contained an autographed picture of Nina. It's signed, "Jerome Arthur, Don't forget to play naked." I have that picture proudly displayed in my shop, and so now I'm a fan.

In my research of Nina, I came across a really good interview on line with Cenk Uygur of *The Young Turks*. What I was really looking for when I found that interview was her appearance with fellow porn star Ona Zee on *The Oprah Winfrey Show*.

I mentioned earlier that I didn't get it when I asked Max what her family thought about what she does. I can't even remember what his response was, but I can see now that whatever it was, it's irrelevant as far as I'm concerned.

After watching the Uygur interview, I think I get it. It's about sex education. She tells Cenk about how she uses the things that Buddhism emphasizes: "personal responsibility, compassionate awareness, mindfulness—absolutely I try to use those things in my day to day life, my own personal sanity and my work as a sex educator, sexual facilitator."

Nina demonstrates all of these traits as a sex educator on her two-disc set, *The Best of Nina Hartley, The Ultimate 6 Hour Superstar Anthology*. In the segments where she's working with women, she actually talks to the camera, and explains what she's doing. The same is true of the two-minute video on her website, nina.com. In that video, wearing her professorial glasses, she says, "A lot of you know, I am a sex educator…," and she wears those glasses in every scene of her two-minute show. Every feature on her website is a numbered lesson. She is indeed a sex educator, and she's really good at it. She's won me over. I'm a fan. I see her work as honest work.

Epilogue

By now I hope the reader sees what I've tried to accomplish with these stories. It isn't really about the people I've profiled. Rather it's about insights into my own life, and how I was influenced by the people I've profiled here. Bottom line—it's six different profiles of me.

About the Author

Jerome Arthur grew up in Los Angeles, California. He lived on the beach in Belmont Shore, a neighborhood in Long Beach, California, for nine years in the 1960s. He and his wife Janet moved to Santa Cruz, California in 1969. These three cities are the settings for his ten novels and one memoir.

Lightning Source UK Ltd.
Milton Keynes UK
UKHW011433030720
365982UK00003B/731